This book

belongs to

_____

_____

_____

for Rae, Rowan,
Michelle & Alvin.
and a
special Thankyou
to Pauliina for the idea.

This paperback edition published in 2004

by Gullane Children's Books

Winchester House,

259-269, Old Marylebone Road

London NW1 5XJ

3 4 5 6 7 8 9 10

Illustrations © Jane Cabrera 2004

The right of Jane Cabrera to be identified as

the illustrator of this work has been asserted

by her in accordance with the Copyright

Designs, and Patents Act, 1988.

If You're Happy and You Know It!

Jane Cabrera

GULLANE CHILDREN'S BOOKS

**Are you feeling happy today?
Join me and my friends
for some sing-along fun . . .**

If you're happy and you know it,
CLAP your hands
If you're happy and you know it,
CLAP your hands
If you're happy and you know it,
And you really want to show it

If you're happy and you know it,
CLAP YOUR HANDS!

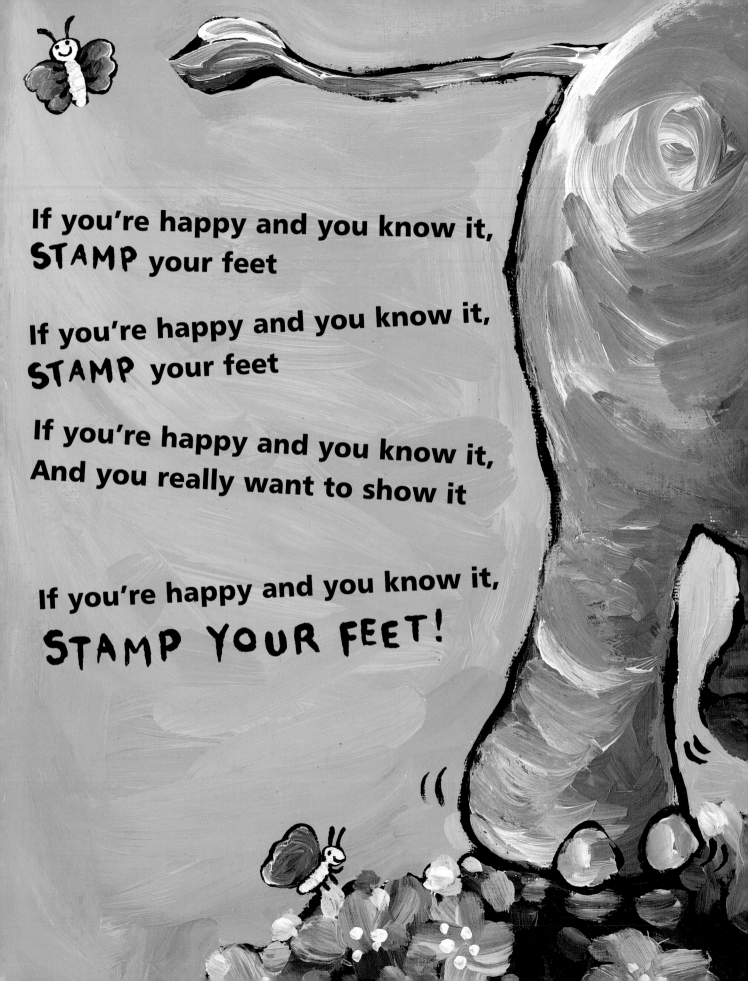

If you're happy and you know it,
STAMP your feet

If you're happy and you know it,
STAMP your feet

If you're happy and you know it,
And you really want to show it

If you're happy and you know it,
STAMP YOUR FEET!

If you're happy and you know it,
NOD your head
If you're happy and you know it,
NOD your head
If you're happy and you know it,
And you really want to show it

If you're happy and you know it,
NOD YOUR HEAD!

If you're happy and you know it,
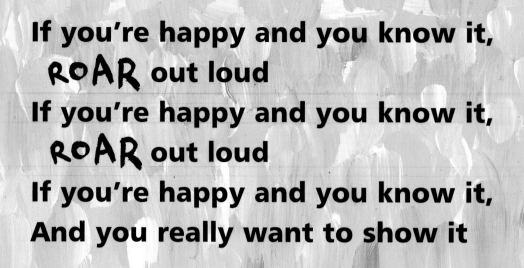 ROAR out loud
If you're happy and you know it,
ROAR out loud
If you're happy and you know it,
And you really want to show it

If you're happy and
you know it,

ROAR
OUT LOUD!

If you're happy and you know it,
SPIN AROUND
If you're happy and you know it,
SPIN AROUND
If you're happy and you know it,
And you really want to show it

If you're happy
and you know it,
SPIN AROUND!

If you're happy and you know it,
go KISS KISS
If you're happy and you know it,
go KISS KISS
If you're happy and you know it,
And you really want to show it

If you're happy and you know it,
go KISS KISS!

If you're happy and you know it, FLAP your arms
If you're happy and you know it, FLAP your arms
If you're happy and you know it,

And you really want to show it
If you're happy and you know it,
FLAP YOUR ARMS!

If you're happy and you know it,
say SQUEAK SQUEAK
If you're happy and you know it,
say SQUEAK SQUEAK
If you're happy and you know it,
And you really want to show it

If you're happy and you know it, say SQUEAK SQUEAK!

If you're happy and you know it, JUMP ABOUT
If you're happy and you know it, JUMP ABOUT
If you're happy and you know it,
And you really want to show it

 If you're happy and you know it,
JUMP ABOUT!

If you're happy and you know it . . .

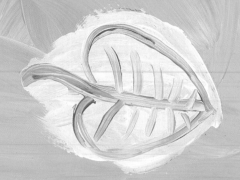

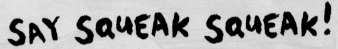

"STAMP YOUR FEET!

NOD YOUR HEAD!"

GO KISS KISS!

FLAP YOUR ARMS!

If you're happy and you know it,
And you really want to show it
If you're happy and you know it,

SHOUT...

We
are!

Other Gullane Children's Books
illustrated by Jane Cabrera

Old Mother Hubbard
JANE CABRERA

A well-loved traditional nursery rhyme about Old Mother Hubbard and her hungry dog who just wants his dinner.

Eggday
JOYCE DUNBAR • JANE CABRERA

Dora the duck decides to hold a best egg competition, but will Pogson the pig, Humphrey the horse and Gideon the goat stand a chance?

Over in the Meadow
JANE CABRERA

Turtles dig, lizards bask, bees buzz and ratties gnaw in this vibrantly illustrated, charming counting rhyme.

My Sister's Hair
SALLY CRABTREE & ROBERTA MATHIESON • JANE CABRERA

Turn the die-cut pages and see Baby's hairdo become increasingly fantastical as her brother's imagination runs riot!

GULLANE
CHILDREN'S BOOKS